When We Are Big

Written by Marilyn Minkoff
Illustrated by Bruce Armstrong

When we are big, what will we be?

What about you?

What about me?

I can be a farmer with a cow and a pig.

You can be a clown and wear a wig.

I can be a cowboy and wear a big hat.

You can be a vet for a dog and a cat.

I can be a dad and have lots of fun.

You can be a runner and jump and run.

I can be a cook with a pot and pan.

You can be the one who will fix the fan.

I can sell things in a shop.

You can tell cars when to stop.

When we are big, what will we be?
We will have to wait and see!